Top 10 Worst™

Creepy Egyptian Mummies

you wouldn't want to meet!

Gareth Stevens
Publishing

Please visit our Web site, **www.garethstevens.com**. For a free color catalog of all our high-quality books, call toll free 1-800-542-2595 or fax 1-877-542-2596.

Library of Congress Cataloging-in-Publication Data

Stewart, David, 1954-
Creepy Egyptian mummies / David Stewart.
   p. cm. — (Top 10 worst)
Includes index.
ISBN 978-1-4339-4080-4 (pbk.)
ISBN 978-1-4339-4081-1 (6 pack)
ISBN 978-1-4339-4079-8 (library binding)
1. Mummies—Egypt—Juvenile literature. I. Title.
DT62.M7S83 2011
932—dc22

                          2010015302

First Edition

Published in 2011 by
Gareth Stevens Publishing
111 East 14th Street, Suite 349
New York, NY 10003

© 2010 The Salariya Book Company Ltd

Series creator: David Salariya
Editor: Stephen Haynes
Illustrations by David Antram

Printed in Heshan, China

CPSIA compliance information: Batch #SS10GS: For further information contact Gareth Stevens,

New York, New York at 1-800-542-2595.

Top 10 Worst™

Creepy

Egyptian Mummies

you wouldn't want to meet!

Illustrated by
David Antram

Written by
David Stewart

Created & designed by
David Salariya

Contents

What is a mummy?

A mummy is a dead body that has been embalmed to preserve it from decay. Most people associate mummies with ancient Egypt, because of horror movies and the high-profile excavation of Tutankhamun.

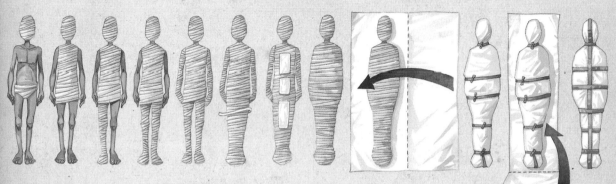

Bandaging the corpse with linen strips. The best-quality linen is placed closest to the body and the roughest is used for the outer layers.

Eternal life

The ancient Egyptians believed in eternal life and the need to provide for the *ka*, one of the dead person's spirits. For this reason, the deceased person's family and friends would leave offerings of food on feast days, or employ priests to do so. The ancient Egyptians believed that saying the name of a dead person was enough to give them everlasting life.

A rich person's mummy might have several magnificent coffins, one inside the other. These would be placed inside a large chest called a sarcophagus.

Are all mummies from ancient Egypt?

Franklin expedition
These British explorers died in 1845. Their bodies were preserved by extreme cold.

Greenland mummies
Six women and two children died around A.D. 1475 and were naturally frozen.

NORTH AMERICA

Shrunken head, Ecuador
Some South American peoples preserved the heads of defeated enemies.

Andean mummy
This child may have been sacrificed to the gods. His body was protected by a cairn of stones.

SOUTH AMERICA

Mummies are not unique to ancient Egypt. Mummies—some created by human skill and some by sheer accident—have existed in many different places and at different times.

Inca mummy, Peru
The ancient Incas are believed to have sacrificed the children of conquered tribes. Cold mountain air preserved the bodies.

Jeremy Bentham *When this British philosopher died in 1832, he asked for his head and skeleton to be preserved. They are now kept in University College, London, England.*

Tollund Man, Denmark *Was he sacrificed, or executed as a criminal? This Iron Age man was hanged or strangled to death and thrown into a peat bog. Acid in the peat preserved the skin.*

ASIA

EUROPE

Lady Dai, China *This Chinese noblewoman died in the second century B.C. Food, cosmetics, and magnificent silk clothes were placed next to her expertly mummified body.*

AFRICA

"Ötzi the iceman" *died more than 5,000 years ago in the Alps between Italy and Austria. His clothes, tools, and weapons were found with him.*

Ötzi and Tollund Man were so well preserved that the people who discovered them thought they were recent murder victims— and called the police.

AUSTRALASIA

Sicilian catacombs, Italy *Bodies were placed in underground passages where they dried out naturally. The oldest dates from A.D. 1599. Later, a chemical treatment was invented which improved the preservation of the remains.*

Mummies of Papua New Guinea *These bodies were preserved by smoking them over a fire.*

How were mummies made?

For centuries in ancient Egypt, only the pharaoh and a few of his aristocratic favorites were mummified. From about 2500 B.C., many other wealthy people were embalmed. Embalming was a religious rite as well as a practical procedure to stop the body from decaying. The finest embalming took 70 days to complete. The first 40 days were devoted to extracting all moisture from the corpse so that no bacteria remained to cause the body to rot.

Vital ingredients

- One freshly scrubbed body
- Incense to fumigate the body
- Natron salt to dry the body
- Palm wine and spices to wash the body inside and out

You wouldn't want to know this:

A metal hook was used to pull out the brain through the nose. The brain was no thought important, and wa thrown away.

It took 15 days to wrap a mummy in 20 layers of linen bandages.

Preserving the innards

The liver, lungs, stomach, and intestines were removed through a slit in the side of the body and stored in canopic jars. Each jar was protected by one of the four sons of the god Horus.

Imsety

The liver was stored in a jar with the human head of the god Imsety on it.

Hapy

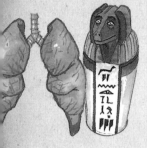

The lungs were kept in a jar with the baboon head of the god Hapy on it.

Duamutef

The stomach was placed in a jar with the jackal head of the god Duamutef on it.

Qebehsenuef

The intestines were stored in a jar with the falcon head of the god Qebehsenuef on it.

Why "mummy"?

"Mummy" comes from m̄miyah, the Arabic word for "bitumen." It used to be thought that mummies were preserved with bitumen—a black, sticky substance found in tar.

The four jars were kept in a specially made wooden chest.

9

No 10

Ginger, the first Egyptian mummy

Nicknamed "Ginger" because of his red hair, he was discovered buried in sand in Gebelein in Egypt. Dating from around 3400 B.C., his body was mummified naturally by the hot and very dry sand that absorbed all the moisture in it. Ginger is ancient Egypt's earliest known mummified body.

Ginger was buried in a curled-up sleeping position. Pots and necklaces that might be useful for the afterlife were buried with him.

Vital statistics

Name: "Ginger"
Discovered: Gebelein, Egypt
Original burial: *c.*3400 B.C.
Current location: British Museum, London, England

You wouldn't want to know this:

Ginger has been in the British Museum in London for more than 100 years. The temperature in the museum is causing Ginger's skin to peel off. The museum's scientists have tried to glue it back on.

Be prepared!
Always expect the very worst

Ötzi the Iceman

Ötzi's arrows and deerskin quiver

Ötzi's flint knife and sheath

Ötzi the Iceman is Europe's oldest mummy, found in September 1991. He dates from the same period as Ginger. Ötzi's nickname comes from the Ötztal Alps where he was found, on the border between Italy and Austria. When bodies are embalmed, their soft parts rot; but Ötzi was naturally mummified by freezing, which preserved his human appearance.

Ötzi's neatly clipped fingernails, his insulated clothing, and his rucksack that held supplies caused his corpse to be mistaken for a recent death when it was first found.

Basket burial

This Egyptian skeleton from 5200 B.C., buried in a basket and interred in a tomb, rotted in the normal way. But other bodies buried in hot, dry sand were naturally dried out and preserved. It did not take the ancient Egyptians long to realize that removing fluid from a corpse aided the preservation process.

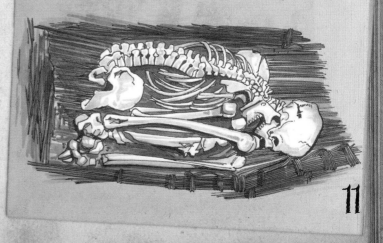

11

№ 9

Tutankhamun

The almost intact tomb of Tutankhamun—the most famous mummy of all time—was discovered in the Valley of the Kings by archaeologist Howard Carter in 1922. Tutankhamun is not a particularly scary-looking mummy—what's more scary is how he was treated by Howard Carter. And, of course, there is the dreaded curse…

Vital statistics

Name: Tutankhamun
Discovered: Valley of the Kings, Egypt
Original burial: 1324 B.C.
Current location: Egyptian Museu Cairo, Egypt

You wouldn't want to know this:

Poor Tutankhamun suffered from a cleft palate, a clubfoot, and various long-term illnesses. He broke his le shortly before his death—but he probably died of malaria.

Solid gold!

Be prepared!
Always expect the very worst

Overdone

So much oil was used in the mummification process that Tutankhamun's flesh stuck to the inside of his coffin. Howard Carter used hot knives to cut up the mummy in order to remove it. The young king's ribs and some other bits are still missing.

Pharaoh's curse?

Lord Carnarvon paid for the archaeological digs which led to the discovery of Tutankhamun's tomb. He died from an infected mosquito bite, four months after the opening of the tomb. Was his death King Tut's revenge? Some people thought so! Yet Howard Carter, who was also present at the opening, lived for another 17 years.

Poked and prodded

In January 2005, Egyptian researchers carried out a CT scan that produced 1,700 images of the mummy. They found that Tutankhamun's left thighbone had been fractured and that the pharaoh's leg became severely infected just before his death.

In Feburary 2010, a study of the pharaoh's DNA proved that Tutankhamun's father was Pharaoh Akhenaten and that his mother was Akhenaten's sister.

No 8

Queen Henuttawy

Queen Henuttawy's mummy was painted yellow. To improve her appearance, her lips and cheeks were painted red and her face was packed with a mixture of fat and soda to restore its fullness. She wears a wig made of strands of black string.

Vital statistics

Name: Henuttawy
Discovered: Thebes, near Luxor, Egypt
Original burial: c.1050 B.C.
Current location: Egyptian Museum, Cairo, Egypt

You wouldn't want to know this:

The embalmers overdid the stuffing on Queen Henuttawy's cheeks and it burst through her skin.

Looking her best

Black string hair

Traces of rouge

Stuffing

Queen Henuttawy was the most important wife of Pinedjem I, Great Priest of Thebes, who ruled Upper Egypt from 1070 to 1032 B.C.

Be prepared! Always expect the very worst

Missing parts

Henuttawy was not the only ancient Egyptian to suffer at the hands of careless embalmers. One mummy's intestines were replaced with a rope. In another, a liver made of cow skin and other organs made from leather and rags were inserted.

Manchester Museum in England has a mummy whose internal organs and legs arc missing. Wooden legs had been substituted under the bandages.

Artistic touches

Some embalmers took great care to create a lifelike body. The shape was improved by adding linen pads, earth, sawdust, and extra bandaging. The skin was colored red for men and yellow for women. False eyes of glass or stone made the mummy look particularly lifelike.

Shabti

Shabti are small figures placed amongst the grave goods in ancient Egyptian tombs. This one was found in the tomb of Henuttawy. If the queen was called upon to work in the afterlife, the shabti would do the work in her place.

There you are— good as new!

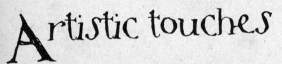

15

No 9

Mixed-up mummy

In late Egyptian history, around 300 B.C., lifelike portraits were placed over the mummy's face. By this time, the appearance of the mummy was much more important than the actual embalming process. X-rays of this mummy showed that it had been interred with someone else's skull between its legs. How did it get there?

Two heads are better than one?

Perhaps the embalmers found that they had an extra head and didn't know whose it was. They may have thought it best to cover up their sloppy workmanship by hiding it in someone else's mummy.

Vital statistics

Name: Not known
Discovered: Valley of the Golden Mummies, Bahariya Oasis, Egypt
Original burial: c.300 B.C.

You wouldn't want to know this:

The tombs at Bahariya Oasis were discovered in 1996 when a donkey put its foot in a hole in the ground. If that donkey hadn't stumbled, we wouldn't know about these mummies.

16

Be prepared!
Always expect the very worst

It's a steal

Linen was valuable because it took so long to weave. That's why it was so popular with tomb robbers. Glass and gold were also sought after, as they could be melted down to make new objects which could not be traced.

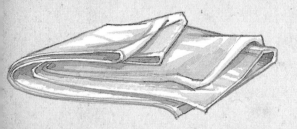

Sometimes, when a tomb had been robbed, priests would quickly gathcr together any broken-up mummies, possibly mixing up some of the body parts.

Punishment

Robbers took advantage of periods when the Egyptian rulers were weak to break into tombs. The gruesome punishment, if they were caught, was impalement—skewering on a wooden pole.

Gold!

What have you got?

No 6

Animal mummies

A nimals, like human beings, have also been preserved by accident or design. Fossils provide evidence of tiny creatures from the first phase of life on Earth. Fossils are not mummies, however, since they mostly consist of minerals that have penetrated and replaced the body.

The Egyptians mummified animals as well as humans. Fakes were sometimes made to sell to tourists, in both ancient and modern times.

Vital statistics

Name: Animal mummies
Discovered: Many places in Egypt
Current location: Egyptian Museum, Cairo, and other museums

You wouldn't want to know this:

Some mummies of sacred bulls contain only the head of the animal. What happened to the rest? Some experts think the priests cooked and ate the meat, then mummified the leftovers.

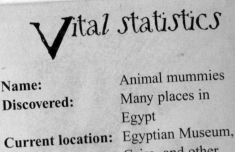

It takes guts to do this job properly.

Sacred animals

The ancient Egyptians believed that some animals were sacred to a particular god. Mummies of that animal would be kept at the god's temple. Crocodiles were sacred to the god Sobek, cats to the goddess Bastet, baboons and ibises to the god Thoth.

101 uses

When European explorers first discovered Egyptian mummies, they did not always treat them with respect. They used them to make medicines, paints, fertilizer, and even torches.

Life after death

Some animals were mummified to provide food for the dead person in the afterlife. Others may have been pets to keep the dead person company. In later times, when Egypt was ruled by the Romans, animal mummies were given as gifts to the gods. They may have been specially bred.

No 5

Queen Nodjmet

The embalmers of Queen Nodjmet's time were trying out new techniques, using padding, wax, and cosmetics to make the mummy more lifelike. Queen Nodjmet's mouth was packed with sawdust and her nose filled with resin. She had artificial eyes made of precious stones, and eyebrows made from real hair. A wig was added to conceal the queen's sparse grey hair and restore her youthful appearance.

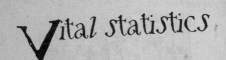

Vital statistics

Name: Nodjmet
Discovered: Thebes, Egypt
Original burial: *c.*1080 B.C.
Current location: Egyptian Museum, Cairo, Egypt

You wouldn't want to know this:

Nodjmet's face was badly scarred when tomb robbers cut through her wrappings in search of valuable jewelry.

Be prepared!
Always expect the very worst

No way to treat a lady!

As well as the cuts to her forehead, cheeks, and nose, Queen Nodjmet's legs were broken and her wrists and collarbone had also been fractured. The priests had to rewrap the body to conceal the damage.

Hacked!

Queen Nodjmet's mummy was found in a set of coffins that were originally made for a man. They were altered for the queen's use. The coffins were badly damaged by blows from an axe-like tool called an adze.

Empty!

The canopic chest of Queen Nodjmet is guarded by a statue of the jackal-headed god Anubis. But the chest is empty. Why? Because by this time the Egyptians had stopped putting the dead person's organs in canopic jars; now they embalmed the organs and put them back inside the body.

No 4

Ramses II

Ramses II, who was crowned pharaoh in his early twenties, ruled Egypt from about 1279 to 1213 B.C. He was originally buried in a tomb of his own in the Valley of the Kings. After the tombs in the Valley were robbed, Ramses' mummy was rewrapped by priests and was moved to the tomb of Queen Inhapy for 72 hours. It was then moved again to the tomb of the high priest Pinudjem II.

How do we know this? All this information was detailed in hieroglyphics on the pharaoh's mummy wrappings.

Vital statistics

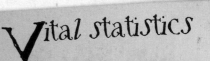

Name:	Ramses II
Discovered:	Valley of the Kings, Egypt
Original burial:	1213 B.C.
Current location:	Egyptian Museum, Cairo, Egypt

You wouldn't want to know this:

It looks as though the embalmers accidentally knocked Ramses' head off (his neck was very scrawny) and used a piece of wood to join it back on.

Better be quick— he'll be on the move again!

Be prepared!
Always expect the very worst

Well travelled

In 1974, Egyptologists saw that the mummy was deteriorating and decided to send it to Paris for examination and treatment. The mummy was issued with a passport that listed his occupation as "King—deceased." Ramses was met at Le Bourget airport near Paris with full military honors.

Ozymandias

The poem "Ozymandias," by Percy Shelley, was inspired by a description of a giant statue of Ramses II. The ruins of the statue stand in the desert, with an inscription that says:

"My name is Ozymandias, king of kings: Look on my works, ye Mighty, and despair!"

The ruined statue shows that even the greatest empires cannot last forever.

Looking inside

Since 1895, X-rays have made it possible to examine the insides of mummies without unwrapping them.

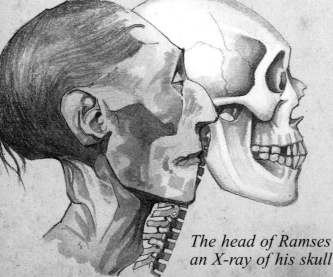

Many new scientific methods are now used to add to our knowledge of ancient Egyptian mummies. These include:

• CT scans (cross-sectional X-rays)
• endoscopy (looking inside the body through a small tube)
• DNA analysis
• radiocarbon dating

The head of Ramses II and an X-ray of his skull

23

No 3

Nesyamun

Nesyamun lived around 1100 B.C. He was Keeper of the Bulls at the great temple of Amun at Karnak. His mummy was found at Deir el-Bahri near Luxor in 1822. He was sent from Egypt to Trieste in Italy in 1823, then on to London to be exhibited in the Egyptian Hall, Piccadilly. But why was Nesyamun mummified with his tongue sticking out?

Vital statistics

Name: Nesyamun
Discovered: Deir el-Bahri, Luxor, Egypt
Original burial: *c.*1100 B.C.
Current location: City Museum, Leeds, England

You wouldn't want to know this:

In 1941, Nesyamun's mummy was damaged by a wartime bomb. He was lucky: all the other mummies at Leeds Museum were completely destroyed.

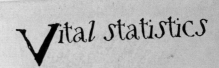

24

Be prepared!
Always expect the very worst

Cause of death

Scientists who examined the body at Leeds in 1828 could not decide how he had died. Was he strangled? Probably not—there are no marks on his neck.

He was examined again in 1989. Did he choke to death after being stung on the tongue by a bee? It's possible.

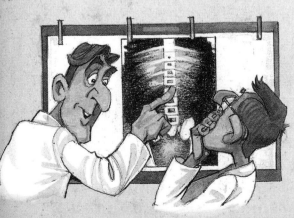

Scientists at Leeds were among the first to use X-rays to study mummies.

A cushy life

We know a lot about Nesyamun's life from the inscriptions on his coffin and the objects buried with him. He was 5 feet 6 inches (1.68 m) tall and died in his mid-forties. He was a *waab* priest, which means that he was allowed to approach the inner sanctum of the great temple of the god Amun. There he performed rituals, recited prayers, and made offerings to Amun. But he only had to work for three months of the year—the rest of his time was his own.

A reconstruction of how Nesyamun may have looked when he was alive

No 2

Seqenenre Tao II

The mummy of Pharaoh Seqenenre was discovered at Deir el-Bahri in 1881. It was unwrapped in 1886. The detailed report of this examination reveals that the pharaoh died from horrific injuries inflicted by clubs and maces. The pharaoh had survived an earlier head wound which may have left him partly paralyzed.

Vital statistics

Name: Seqenenre Tao II
Discovered: Deir el-Bahri, Luxor, Egypt
Original burial: *c.*1558 B.C.
Current location: Egyptian Museum, Cairo, Egypt

You wouldn't want to know this:

The embalmers had to do a rush job on the pharaoh's body because it had already begun to rot before they started work.

26

Be prepared!
Always expect the very worst

French Egyptologist Gaston Maspero unwraps the mummy

From Gaston Maspero's report:

"A blow from an axe must have severed part of his left cheek, exposed the teeth, fractured the jaw, and sent him senseless to the ground."

Who was he?

Seqenenre Tao II is sometimes referred to as "the Brave." He fought against a neighboring people called the Hyksos, who had been enemies of the Egyptians for centuries. His son Ahmose carried on the fight against the Hyksos, and eventually defeated them.

Was Seqenenre Tao II killed in battle against the Hyksos, or was he murdered? We don't know. But, judging by the state of the body, he must have been left where he fell for some time.

Seqenenre Tao II was pharaoh for only a short time, but he did find time to build a mud-brick palace at a place now known as Deir el-Ballas.

"Another blow must have seriously injured the skull, and a dagger or javelin has cut open the forehead on the right side, a little above the eye."

"The hair is thick, rough and matted; the face had been shaved on the morning of his death."

An axe, a dagger, and a mace (battle club). Seqenenre Tao II was probably killed by weapons like these.

No 1

The "screaming mummy"

In 1886, Gaston Maspero, the head of the Egyptian Antiquities Service, was unwrapping one of the many mummies of kings and queens that had been moved in ancient times to hide them from grave robbers. When this mummy's plain, undecorated coffin was opened, Maspero made a shocking discovery. There, wrapped in a sheepskin or goatskin, lay the body of a young man, his face screaming in agony, his hands and feet tightly bound.

Vital statistics

Name: Prince Pentewere (possibly)

Discovered: Valley of the Kings, Egypt

Original burial: *c.*1155 B.C.

Current location: Egyptian Museum, Cairo, Egypt

You wouldn't want to know this:

Sheep and goats were considered unclean by the Egyptians. Wrapping a body in the skin of an unclean animal was a dreadful insult.

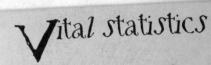

Ça alors!
(Good Lord!)

Be prepared!
Always expect the very worst

Who was the mystery man?

One theory is that the "screaming mummy" is Prince Pentewere, son of Pharaoh Ramses III. Pentewere and his mother, Queen Tiy, were involved in a plot to murder the pharaoh and put Pentewere on the throne.

Ramses III

Is he really screaming?

Probably not. The gaping jaw may have been caused by the head falling back on the work table as the body was being mummified. Later Egyptian embalmers worked out ways to prevent this from happening.

Unnamed for eternity

A papyrus scroll records how the plot was quickly discovered and the plotters were executed. But it seems that Pentewere was not killed along with the others. Because of his royal blood, he was allowed to commit suicide by drinking poison—a less shameful death.

He was buried without a grave marker, so his name would never be known—a punishment that would last for all eternity.

Drink it up!

29

Glossary

Afterlife The life of the soul after the death of the body.

Archaeology The study of the remains of past civilizations.

Cairn A heap of stones intended as a memorial.

Canopic chest A wooden box in which canopic jars are kept.

Canopic jars A set of four jars used to store the preserved organs of a mummy.

Catacombs Underground tunnels where dead bodies are stored.

CT Computed tomography—a method of creating a 3-D image from X-ray photographs.

Deceased Dead.

DNA Deoxyribonucleic acid, a genetic material found in all living cells that controls how they grow and develop.

Egyptologist A historian who studies ancient Egypt.

Embalming A process in which fluids are removed from a dead body and replaced with chemicals to prevent decay.

Excavation The process of digging into the ground to search for archaeological remains.

Fossil The buried remains of a plant or animal, turned into stone by a natural process over thousands or millions of years.

Fumigate To purify an object or a place by using smoke to kill insects and bacteria.

Grave goods Possessions that are buried with a dead person so that they can be used in the afterlife.

Hieroglyphics A system of writing used by the ancient Egyptians, especially for sacred texts.

Ibis A long-legged bird with a long, curved beak.

Incense A substance which is burned to produce sweet-smelling smoke.

Inscription A text that is painted or carved on a wall or other object.

Interred Buried in the ground.

Iron Age The period of prehistory after the invention of iron. It occurred at different times in different places.

Mace A club used as a fighting weapon.

Malaria A disease carried by mosquitoes, which can be fatal if modern medicines are not available.

Mummification The process of turning a dead body into a mummy.

Natron A natural form of salt the ancient Egyptians used to dry out the moisture from a dead body.

Papyrus A kind of reed the Egyptians used to make a writing material similar to paper.

Peat bog An area of wet ground filled with decaying vegetable matter.

Pharaoh A king or queen of ancient Egypt.

Prehistory The time before written documents were created.

Radiocarbon dating A method of finding out how old things are by measuring the amount of radioactive carbon they contain. It works only on animal or plant materials.

Sacrifice To kill a person or animal as a gift to the gods.

Sanctum A part of a temple that is considered especially sacred.

Sarcophagus A large, chest-shaped coffin, which may have smaller coffins inside it.

Scroll A rolled-up sheet of paper or papyrus.

Shabti A small figure of a servant. Ancient Egyptians believed that these figures could work for their owners in the afterlife.

Index